Nineteenth-Century Houses
in Western New York

Century-old cast-iron dogs in Westfield.

Side porch and balcony of Atherly
house in Ashville.

Nineteenth-Century Houses in Western New York

By
Jewel Helen Conover

State University of New York
College at Fredonia

PHOTOGRAPHS BY THE AUTHOR

STATE UNIVERSITY OF NEW YORK PRESS
ALBANY

First Edition
First Printing 1966
Second Printing 1971

Published by State University of New York Press
Thurlow Terrace, Albany, New York 12201

© 1966 The Research Foundation of State University of New York

ISBN 0-87395-017-8 (clothbound)
ISBN 0-87395-117-4 (microfiche)
LC Catalog Card Number 66-63788

Printed in the United States of America

For Mother and Father,
Mae and Charlotte.

Foreword

For years I have been nattering about the lack of attention paid to the marvelously varied and highly imaginative architecture which characterizes almost every village and crossroads of upstate New York. Now, all of a sudden we are in the midst of a happy, wide-eyed era of recognition. This spring the New York State Council on the Arts published an exciting and provocative volume called *Architecture Worth Saving in Onondaga County,* by Harley J. McKee and his associates at Syracuse University School of Architecture. A few weeks later came *Capitol Story,* published by the State of New York and brilliantly written by Cecil R. Roseberry, a delightfully illustrated volume devoted to that marvelous behemoth in Albany which is our State Capitol. In the works, again under the aegis of the Council on the Arts, are books on the buildings of Albany and Rensselaer Counties and another on Wayne County. And now, published appropriately by the State University of New York, comes Miss Conover's study of the homes of Chautauqua County.

Generations from now, when the social historians tell of the cultural rediscoveries of these years, and note how in the middle sixties we Yorkers began to look at our landmarks and find them good, they will say enviously, "How exciting to have lived in those times." And how correct they will be. Chautauqua County is the far western toe of New York, more westerly than Buffalo, even—the last toehold of civilization before you move into the Near East. It provides seventy miles of shoreline for Lake Erie, thousands of gallons of grape juice, furniture from the good Swedish craftsmen of Jamestown, poltergeists and other-worldly messages at the Spiritualist colony at Lily Dale, summer culture at Chautauqua, and well-trained teacher candidates, students of the arts and of the sciences, and budding musicians at the State University College at Fredonia. It is a gentle, rolling countryside and, like the rest of New York State, it is full of well-built, interesting homes done in a myriad of styles and intermarriages of styles.

And this is what Miss Conover writes about so tellingly—the houses and their relationship to the landscape and history that created them. She writes of the simplest stone and wooden frontier houses that have come down to us, the noble neoclassic mansions, the carpenter gothics with their gossamer porches and decorations, the great, solid, arrogant Italianate villas, the breasty Queen Annes with their roundnesses, and of an octagon, still cherishing its octagon barn, the epitome of midnineteenth century pseudoscience playing with building blocks. Here is a cross section of one hundred years of American architecture; here also is a cross section of what can be seen in county after county in the Empire State; for whatever its individual characteristics, Chautauqua County is architecturally typical of all the counties south of the Adirondacks.

You will find a record here, not only of the buildings themselves, but of the accoutrements and embellishments that are also a delight: the iron dogs, the fountains, urns, gazebos, and summerhouses, and those lacy grilles that embellished the low, upper windows.

I don't want to hold you from the pleasures that lie in the pages ahead, but I warn you that once you have finished reading them, and digesting these photographs, you will never again go blindly along our New York roads, through our towns and villages, without seeing with clearer eyes what you have only half seen heretofore. And then the bug will bite you and you will want to own one of these houses—to live in, to raise a family in, to grow old in—to save, to protect from the ravages of highway departments, supermarkets, and gas station builders. You'll get the feeling that here is a part of the precious America we don't want to lose, at any price. Go ahead now and read what follows, but I did warn you.

—LOUIS C. JONES

New York State Historical Association
Cooperstown, New York

Contents

Introduction

In the southwestern corner of New York State, particularly in Chautauqua County, are some of the finest examples of nineteenth-century American domestic architecture to be found anywhere in this country. The architectural styles that were introduced into the United States during the century—and the nameless productions based on many of them—are all to be found there in a comparatively limited area, and I have photographed most of them.

Wayne Andrews, in his beautiful book *Architecture in America,* says of his pictures: "In my judgment a good photograph is not a record of a building. It is an invitation to the beholder to go and see the building for himself." [1] This is true, also, of my photographs; but in addition, I emphasize that each picture is an urgent reminder that these defenseless examples of our American heritage should be preserved. The things I have told about each of the houses I have made quite personal, too, rather than entirely cool and statistical.

The settling and developing of the countryside is traced briefly in these pages because villages and, of course, dwellings are built along roads and close to the railroads and navigable waterways. Immigration to Chautauqua started, conveniently enough, at the very beginning of the nineteenth century. It is necessary, of course, to know about the people who came, the privations and joys they experienced, and the kind of work they did, in order to appreciate fully the homes that they built.

My discussion of the domestic architecture that prevailed, especially in the eastern part of the United States, follows chronologically according to the introduction of the styles into this country during the century. Examples of each of them will be found among the photographs in Section IV—although this collection is only a sampling of the total number of the houses in the county that have character and charm. Pictures of all the houses found in each village are grouped together so that one may know what to look for when visiting these places, and the towns are grouped in a logical geographical order.

Actually, who can accurately classify these mansions into architectural styles or trace them reliably to sources of inspiration? Seldom was a professional architect employed; in earlier days domestic architecture was a personal achievement, and each builder interpreted a style in his own way. We should preserve these houses, for the ones that survive are monuments, in many cases extraordinarily imaginative ones, to the ingenuity of our forebears as craftsmen and builders. Furthermore, they are evidences of our recent ancestors' concern for the future, for, certainly they are solidly built—to endure.

Often, unfortunately, very little is known or remembered about either a house, its builder, or its architect—if it had one. In this hunt for architectural treasure, however, one studies styles and, of course, deviations from known styles, although it is always the house, itself, that matters. Thomas E. Tallmadge, in his book *The Story of Architecture in America,* says, "A favorite and cruel amusement of the modern critic is to run to earth the old doorways, mantelpieces, etc., of the venerable carpenters and show from what particular designs they were filched." [2] Happily, this is not always true. Finding the houses and searching out their heritages inevitably changes any thought of critical condescension to one of sincere admiration for the fearless ingenuity of the long-forgotten builders.

Reflected in the designs, then, we find perfectly respectable inheritances from many countries and periods, and from the greatest architects of all time: Samuel McIntire, Thomas Jefferson, Charles Bulfinch, Andrew Jackson Downing, Alexander Jackson Davis, James Renwick, Jr., Richard Upjohn, and, of course, later, Richard M. Hunt and Henry Hobson Richardson.

Among these architectural designs are lovely Greek Revival houses inspired by the marble temples of Athens. Here they are transformed into distinguished buildings of wood or even of brick. Many that are called English Gothic have purely American embellishments; others reflect the styles of French chateaux, Italian villas and palaces, Swiss chalets, and English manor houses. Toward the latter part of the century the houses become truly elaborate, sometimes confused, and the Parisian mansard styles are often quite homely. There are incredibly eclectic combinations of some of these—of undeniably dubious taste.

But one should not overlook the fact that it has been the fashion to call at least some of them "terrible." Take another look, this time with respect, appreciation—even with affection—and you will find a pervasive atmosphere of sincerity and honesty about them. They have dignity, a certain majesty, and timelessness.

Many houses have been preserved or restored to their original grandeur. Unfortunately, too many are sad sights of hopeless neglect and decay. But all of them are, nonetheless, a segment of our history. Therefore, aside from the value of preserving their beauty and originality, they are important in tracing the development of our civilization. We are what we are because of our past. These houses are part of the record.

It is a pleasure to remember the many people to whom I feel gratitude for help and information received during the more than two years I have worked on this subject. Not only is Chautauqua County rich in distinguished architecture, but the people whom I met and talked with there are wonderful beyond measure. To them I give my heartfelt thanks and my hope that we shall meet again.

I am indebted to Harley J. McKee and Douglas H. Shepard for the valuable suggestions they gave me after reading the manuscript, and to Howard Blanding for technical assistance with my photographs.

I am particularly grateful to Louis C. Jones whose enthusiasm was of vital importance to me right from the beginning, and to Oscar E. Lanford whose help and encouragement have brought the work to its culmination. Finally, it is good to realize how fortunate I am that my sister, Charlotte D. Conover, who read and corrected the manuscript and advised me in numberless ways, is both scholarly and generous.

JEWEL HELEN CONOVER

Fredonia, New York
1965

Nineteenth-Century Houses
in Western New York

Late nineteenth-century fountain placed in Barker Commons in Fredonia in 1900.

1

The Countryside

Gazebo in Brocton.

The land in the southwestern corner of New York State was heavily forested at the beginning of the nineteenth century. Great old trees: hemlock, white pine and maple; oak, willow, chestnut, hickory, basswood, butternut, walnut, tulip, sycamore, cherry, and many others, flourished there—a treasure in timber that later turned to gold.

Wild animals roamed the forests, with the bear and wolf so destructive to the early settlers and to their domestic animals that the combined bounty eventually offered by the State and towns for the scalp of a full-grown wolf amounted to a munificent fifty dollars. This comparatively easy money, however, was somewhat reduced when it was discovered that payment was being made occasionally for dogs' heads instead of for those of wolves, and in view of the case of the resourceful farmer who raised wolves and then killed them for the bounty.

The earliest known Indian inhabitants were the Eries, "Nation of the Cat." In the middle of the seventeenth century they were driven out (or killed off) by the Iroquois, who had the advantage of being the first Indians to establish trading relations with the Dutch of the Hudson Valley. They obtained steel knives, hatchets, axes, cast-iron kettles, and—most important—guns and ammunition from Dutch traders. The unfortunate Eries were eventually replaced by the Seneca and Onondaga tribes of the Iroquois Nation. Remains of Indian camps and villages have been excavated along Lake Erie. In Gerry, in 1887, an ossuary was opened which contained the bones of about fifty people, and another was found in the heart of the Chautauqua Assembly grounds.

This land was sparsely populated by white men, then, when it became Chautauqua County in 1808. But it was a lovely land with its gently rolling hills and valleys, its magnificent forests, a long northwestern boundary following the shores of Lake Erie, and smaller lakes scattered throughout the countryside. By 1825, however, fifteen towns had been organized and the "County of Chautauque (sic)" had a population of 20,639—and by 1825, too, some of the handsomest houses shown in Section IV had been built.

Important in the early development of the area were the roads that made it accessible, which were mainly trails tramped by the Indians and paths cut through the wilderness by the white men. The earliest local one, a portage road, was built by the French in 1755 from Barcelona on Lake Erie to Chautauqua Lake. Somewhat later two roads were authorized by the legislature: one to be four rods wide, connecting Canadaway (now Fredonia) and Perry, seventy-five miles to the east; and another to run from Fredonia to Buffalo. In 1816 David Thomas traveled west through Canadaway, along the Lake Erie Beach Road, which ran parallel to the shore—a few miles inland. In his journal he reported that there were thirty houses in the village when he was there, about twenty-two of which, he thought, had been built within that year.[3]

The State was aware of the vital need for roads, and by 1825 the Albany-Schenectady Turnpike and the Great Western Turnpike had been built by chartered turnpike companies, who collected tolls to pay for them. Extensions reached to the western edge of the State. Route 5, running along the shore of Lake Erie, and Route 20, farther inland, follow approximately the course of the earliest roads westward.

In 1837 a "highway" was built from Fredonia to Jamestown. Labor—hard, back-breaking labor—was cheap in those days. Three men cut a road one rod wide, twenty-one miles long, from Gerry to the Cattaraugus County line. It took them three months to clear and make it passable, and they were paid ten dollars per mile.

Many writers have described the picturesque sights and sounds of the midcentury migration westward: the Conestogas and prairie schooners packed heavily with household goods, rolling into the sunset on broad-rimmed wheels; the notion-stocked caravans of peddlers; the tinkers and itinerant artists, the cattle herded by drovers along dusty trails, and the fast overland stages carrying passengers and mail behind three- and four-horse teams. These sights were familiar to residents of Chautauqua County, some of whom joined the hopeful trek.

As early as 1825 a line of stagecoaches, most of them drawn by four horses, made daily trips from Dunkirk through Westfield and on to Erie, connecting with a schedule of lake steamers for the transportation of mail and passengers. Another stage made regular runs between Fredonia and Jamestown.

The transportation advantages of the waterways of the Great Lakes, of the Mississippi and Ohio Rivers, played a vital part in the development of the area. During the nineteenth century, navigation on Lake Erie and the other Great Lakes was extremely active. Steamboats carrying passengers and cargo passed each other daily except during the ice-bound winter months. Shipbuilding boomed in Dunkirk, Silver Creek, and Irving. The first paddlewheel steamboat to make regular trips was called "Walk-in-the-Water"—reminiscent, certainly, of descriptive Indian names—and patriotic Dunkirk turned out *en masse* to cheer her arrival from Buffalo on her maiden voyage in 1818.

The gas-illuminated lighthouse at Barcelona Harbor, called the tallest gaslight in the world, was built in 1825 and served for many years as a welcome guide to these ships at night. Natural gas had been discovered in nearby Fredonia in 1821, and this town was the first one in the country to put it to economic use. When Lafayette visited Fredonia in 1825 he remarked on the brightly lighted town. Certainly, after the dimness of candles and oil lamps, the brilliance of gas lights was dazzling.

Natural gas was first observed bubbling up in the water in Canadaway Creek and then in Lake Erie, close to the shore at Sheridan, Van Buren, and near Barcelona. In 1873 William Risley (who, incidentally, lived in a fine Greek Revival house in Fredonia) described the amazing phenomenon of "burning the creek." This improbable achievement was accomplished by piling stones in the water to surface level, over the bubbles of gas, stacking dry sticks onto this platform, and setting them afire.[4]

A major engineering feat opened another pathway to western New York when the Erie Canal was completed in 1825. Buffalo and Albany now had a direct route to New York City and the Atlantic Ocean. This forward step was acclaimed in a series of colorful celebrations marking the opening of the canal. DeWitt Clinton, with a large party, made the first trip from Buffalo to New York, their canal-boat, the *Seneca Chief,* carrying a barrel of Lake Erie water. Leaving Buffalo on October 26, 1825, they were greeted by welcoming crowds who toasted and applauded them all along the way.

On November 4, upon reaching New York and the coast, the travelers were cheered wildly, flags waved, bands played and Clinton ". . . in pursuance of arrangements marked with peculiar splendor and magnificence . . ."[5] dramatically emptied the barrel of Lake Erie water into the blue waves of the Atlantic Ocean. On November 25, another elegant keg, labeled "Neptune's Return to Pan" and full of salt water from the ocean, was brought to Buffalo and poured into Lake Erie, also with great ceremony.

Oak and pine were used for building schooners and canalboats; basswood, pine, and hemlock were fuel for running them; rafts were built and ambitious lumbering operations established—finally, great bonfires of hardwood burned night and day, to reduce valuable timber to the ashes that were leached to turn them into pearlash. Thus the depletion of the virgin forests in Chautauqua County began and was to continue.

It is difficult now to realize the rapidity with which tremendous expansion came about everywhere in New York State during the nineteenth century, once it got started. An early stage that ran regularly between Albany and Canandaigua twice a week took four days to make the trip. In 1807 a connecting run between Canandaigua and Buffalo was established to make the trip at least once a week from July 1 to October 1, to carry at one time no more than seven passengers (exceptions made only with their unanimous consent), plus fourteen pounds of baggage each, the fare not to exceed six cents per mile per passenger! Compare this early traveling with the fact that the Erie Railroad, not very long thereafter and before the middle of the century, carried over one million people during its first year of existence. These were the years, too, of great population growth in New York State, from 1,049,458 in 1820 to 1,724,033 in 1840— an increase of 674,575 in only twenty years.

The year 1851 marked the completion of 483 miles of this railway across New York State to Dunkirk; and the village of Dunkirk, disappointed that it had not been chosen to be the western terminus of the Erie Canal, really extended itself on that great day in May. The description of the occasion in Andrew Young's *History of Chautauqua County,* published in 1875, is delightful:

> This was a joyous occasion, not only to the citizens of this county, but to thousands in every county in the "southern tier." These "sequestered counties," as they had long been called, having participated but slightly in the benefits of the "grand canal," were at length favored with a "road to market." The day was highly auspicious, and many thousands were attracted by the fame of the expected guests, and the novelty of the anticipated spectacle. The village of Dunkirk presented a gay appearance, from the flags and streamers with which the hotels and private houses were decorated. On the depot were the flags of three nations; the stars and stripes gracefully floating above the tricolor of the French republic and the red cross of St. George.
>
> At about 11 o'clock, the Queen City arrived from Buffalo, and soon after, in succession, the Niagara, the Empire State, the Empire, the Key Stone State, and the United States steamer Michigan, took positions in the harbor. Gov. Hunt and suite arrived from Buffalo on one of the boats, and received his friends at the American hotel. The train from New York, expected at 1:30 P.M., did not arrive until about 4, when the locomotive "Dunkirk" came in as a pioneer, followed, soon after, by the long expected "iron horse" from New York city, amid the ringing of bells and shouts of thousands. The train consisted of twelve passenger cars, bearing a long row of banners which had been presented along the line. Among the guests in the train were President Fillmore; Daniel Webster, secretary of state; Wm. A. Graham, secretary of the navy; Nathan K. Hall, postmaster-general; John J. Crittenden, attorney-general; Senators Seward and Fish; Daniel S. Dickinson; Ex-Gov. Marcy; Senator Douglas of Ill.; Christopher Morgan, sec. of state of New York, and others.[6]

It is a matter of record, too, that President Fillmore rode in on a flat-top car comfortably seated in a rocking chair.

This was another event that Dunkirk enthusiastically celebrated. The town staged an elaborate parade with a Cornet Band, served a sumptuous "collation," speeches, of course, were made by nearly everybody, and the exciting day ended with a glittering display of fireworks and bonfires.

Other rail lines, spur and short lines were promoted throughout the State and between villages. They flourished and died. Electric lines later in the century followed the same patterns. These, too, have been replaced and their history has been almost obliterated by the recent gaudy saga of autos, trucks, buses, and airplanes. But the early stagecoaches, steamboats, and trains were also gaudy in their day, and this is good to remember; and the well-loved "interurban" electric cars did much to make neighbors of towns separated by distance.

Emigration westward as early as 1820 along the Old Erie Road in northern Chautauqua County brought people to this area and, of course, through and beyond it. A great impetus toward its settlement, however, resulted from promotions of that enterprising Dutch organization, the Holland Land Company, active not only in western New

York State but also in part of Pennsylvania. After acquiring the land, the company planned town sites and sold the properties to settlers at reasonable rates and terms. The central office of the Holland Land Company in 1801 was Batavia, New York. The company's office in Mayville still stands, and there is another in Westfield.

Slowly at first, but with steady persistence, the county was settled; it blossomed and flourished. The appearance of the landscape changed —land was cleared, the soil was fertile, trees were plentiful, and farming and lumbering operations prospered; villages grew. Thus lightly, in this mechanized age, one passes over the statement, "land was cleared." In 1875 Andrew Young wrote: "To clear the soil of its timber required an amount of hard labor of which many of its present occupants have no adequate conception. Many now living on the hard-earned fortunes of their pioneer fathers and grandfathers, could not be induced to enter upon a similar course of labor." [7] How very true! And then he describes in detail the heartbreaking labor involved.

Chautauqua became a productive and beautiful county, however, as the nineteenth century rolled along. With lumbering came great furniture manufacturers, notably in Jamestown, which is still famous for this industry. Besides successful farming there were thriving dairy farms producing exceptionally fine cheese and butter, and many other industries (to be discussed later) brought modest wealth to the towns. The harvest of small fruits and vegetables and the extensive vineyards along the shores of Lake Erie caused the fall season in Chautauqua County to be painted with an artist's paradise of colors —purple and gold, crimson, green and yellow—brilliant against the ultramarine of the waters of Lake Erie and of Chautauqua, Cassadaga, and Findley Lakes: haunted by the lonely honking of great flocks of geese flying south for the winter. In these things the years have brought no change.

The climate varies somewhat, with the differences in elevation in Chautauqua County. The low land along Lake Erie has slightly milder winters than the hills and higher valleys. Nowhere, however, are the winters easy. Blizzards loaded with heavy snows sweep down across the lake from Canada, and great ice dunes pile up along the shores. The soft and gentle springs that follow are always welcome; the summer weather is ideal. The country, then, was beautiful as well as prosperous, and the people there had houses that were well built because of the weather, well planned for comfortable living for the large families—houses whose designs still reflect the prosperity, the dignity, and the pride of the owners.

II

The People and the Villages

1870 Bandstand in Ellington.

The first white settler in Chautauqua County at the end of the eighteenth century seems not to have appreciated the possibilities of that glorious wilderness. He stayed only three years. More farsighted people immediately followed him, however, and by 1801 there were small scattered settlements throughout the county; in 1810 the population was 2381, in 1825 more than twenty thousand people were living in fifteen organized towns, and in 1875 over sixty thousand were prospering in twenty-six towns.

Most of the people who came during the nineteenth century were New Englanders. In fact, "Vermont Settlement" was the first name given to Gerry. Others came up the Hudson from New York and New Jersey; also, with no immigration quota, the door of America was open to Europeans—and they came eagerly, some of them directly to Chautauqua County.

"Directly," however, is relative. In 1850, for instance, groups from Sweden settled in Jamestown, New York, their trip following this pattern: After leaving their Swedish homes they waited in the port of Gothenburg for passage on a vessel sailing for America, the travelers bringing, of course, enough provisions for the entire trip. The ships were small and crowded, and sea travel, at best, was primitive; but these hardy immigrants somehow survived the eleven weeks it took to cross the rough Atlantic. In New York City they waited around again for steamship passage to Albany; and from there, eventually, they embarked on a canalboat, which would take two weeks more to get to Buffalo. Here they transferred to a lake steamer for the five-hour sail to Dunkirk where, finally, they were obliged to hire horse-drawn wagons or oxcarts for the last slow lap of the painful journey, west or south, to their final destination. This, indeed, was a distressingly long and difficult introduction to their new country; but they came to make a better life than the one they had left, most of them succeeding.

From England and from Ireland's Counties Kerry and Cork they came, usually in small numbers; and from Germany, Denmark, Italy, Poland, Greece, even from Albania. Industrious and happy, they became fine citizens and mingled successfully with the Americans already established here.

We have little appreciation of the many hardships faced and overcome by the pioneers, how expensive it was in time and, even by our standards, in money. In the wilderness, for instance, by far the most precious possession—indeed the most necessary of all—was an axe; and it was worth twenty-five dollars in cash. In 1846 historian Emory F. Warren wrote: "It was indispensable to the pioneer. Without it he could do nothing. His track through the wilderness was marked by it, and his roads opened. His first efforts at building were made with it, and the food for his cattle furnished from the tops of the forest trees, which his sturdy arm felled for that purpose." [8]

The men often had to cut their way through dense forests, following the marked trees, for such necessary supplies as flour, costing as high as thirty dollars a barrel, for pork from eighteen to thirty dollars a barrel, and for salt at twenty-five dollars a keg. When enough land had been cleared on which to raise grain, and before gristmills were near enough for use, the farmers rubbed corn into hominy and then ground it by pounding with a hominy block. By 1804 both a gristmill and a sawmill were in operation on the Chautauqua Creek near Barcelona, but getting to them, of course, was another matter. The men hunted and fished too, all this being required just to exist. "But," says Mr. Warren philosophically, "with these privations, came appetite, and health, and enjoyment, without any of the diseases incident to the indulgences in the luxuries of more modern times." [9]

Clearing the wilderness, settling and cultivating the land, building a livable house, did not mean that life would be easy from then on for these people. While the Holland Land Company was generous with terms in dealing with purchases of land, the pioneers often had difficulty in meeting even the small periodical payments for it. After ten years, if too little, or if nothing had been paid, an "increase of purchase money" was added to the original price. The company sometimes made concessions by accepting cattle or grain in part payment, although this was not acceptable unless a good market was located within a reasonable distance. It also offered an appreciable discount on the price of the land if cash was paid at the time of purchase. But sometimes a settler was unable to raise even as small a downpayment as ten dollars on a tract, failed to make any payments at all, and finally, after a struggle to live, had to forfeit both the land and his years of labor upon it.

The War of 1812 was a devastating experience for these men and their families. A regiment organized in the county in 1811 was ill-equipped and untrained, and in the field the troops were forced to exist without proper living quarters. Often they were without food. When war was declared the men had to leave homes that were barely established, families that were in need or actually in danger, cattle insufficiently fed and uncared for. There are records that describe how, along Lake Erie, armed sailors from the British fleet came ashore to take whatever they could find—or to desert. Chautauqua County citizens were especially jubilant, then, when Commodore Oliver Hazard Perry was victorious over the British fleet on Lake Erie in 1813. The end of the war in 1814 saw the return of the men to their homes and to the continued struggle for existence through the depression that followed it.

Another burden in the early days was the continual fear of marauding Indians and, even more, of wild animals. When George H. Frost settled in Cherry Creek in 1823, historian Charles J. Shults tells us: "But few settlers had reached the town at that time and the forests were with a few small exceptions, unbroken, and bears, wolves and deer roamed unmolested. The wolves in particular were a terror to the inhabitants and no one ventured from their houses at night without a torch or weapon for protection." [10] Their howling, near and far, particularly at night, was, without a doubt, terrifying; equally frightening were the pumas and wildcats. These and the black bear were a constant menace to the safety of domestic animals, while adding to the problem of existence were hungry raccoons that made raids upon the crops.

Section IV will show that lovely homes were being built in spite of war and other hardships—and it was inevitable, too, that some enterprises would flourish and prosper *because* of the war.

In 1845 a third of the county was under cultivation and, if one is interested in statistics which in themselves reveal much social history, here they are:

> [Chautauqua County] then contained a population of 23,453 males, of whom 10,159 were entitled to vote, and 23,095 females; 129 persons of color and 9,552 children between 5 and 16 years of age. The year preceding (1844) the territory produced 268,261 bushels of wheat, 32,833 of barley, 313,121 of corn, 3,158 of rye, 448,835 of oats, 20,000 of buckwheat, 3,183 of beans, 28,746 of peas, 6,815,869 of potatoes, 22,143 of turnips and 129,749 pounds of flax. It then contained 66,885 neat cattle, 25,024 cows, from which 2,130,303 pounds of butter, and 974,474 pounds of cheese were made the preceding year; 10,507 horses, 235,403 sheep, 73 churches, 4 academies, 307 common schools, 43 grist mills, 206 saw mills, 106 clergymen, 61 attornies and 90 physicians.[11]

No teachers were catalogued, although one of the first concerns of the people upon settling a community was to establish a school. In any event there certainly were teachers, the early pedagogues being male; and they had to be tough. Dr. Gilbert Hazeltine in 1887 reminisces about them:

> In these districts the first thing to be done at the commencement of each winter's school was to break all rules and whip the school master. It took the stoutest, double-breasted [sic] fellows in the country to manage one of these schools, and teachers for them were quite as frequently chosen for their bodily strength as for their mental qualifications. . . .[12]

Higher education came with the incorporation of the Fredonia Academy by the legislature in 1824 (now the State University of New York College at Fredonia) followed by academies in Jamestown, Dunkirk, Westfield, Mayville, Ellington, and Forestville. Classical studies were among the requirements in order to obtain allocations of money from the State Literature Fund, and these studies included a minimum reading of the first book of Virgil's *Aeneid*. In order to build the academy, enterprising Fredonia citizens not only pledged small amounts of cash but they contributed labor, such as carpentry and cabinetwork, and timber, grain, meat, clapboards, nails, glass, a cow, hay, and twenty dollars worth of shoes—an aggregate equivalent to $890.[13]

The Chautauqua Assembly, started at Lake Chautauqua in 1874, was actually the introduction of the summer school into this country. Initially, it was for religious studies, but shortly it expanded to include groups studying art, music, drama, literature, languages; then important literary figures and other celebrities came to lecture or to perform: statesmen, scientists, travelers, musicians, actors; and orchestras, bands, and choruses gave great outdoor concerts.

Chautauqua became a self-contained community attracting thousands of visitors to take advantage of these cultural activities—and the social and athletic events—in an ideal summer vacation spot complete with waterfront sports. Even an excursion steamer cruised on Lake Chautauqua and made regular stops at the Chautauqua Assembly grounds pier.

Picturesque houses were built by vacationers and students who returned there year after year; and close to some of the homes, platforms were constructed on which to place tents to accommodate visitors. At first the crowds that came lived in hundreds of such tents for the short time that they would remain; but with the increasing popularity of summer-long vacations and the extended studies offered there, guest houses and hotels were built. These are splendid nineteenth-century buildings—they have a distinct "Chautauqua Assembly" atmosphere, and they have to be seen to be appreciated.

Throughout the county people throve, villages grew. Lumber and gristmills were in every town. Farming, dairying, great orchards and vineyards developed and prospered, the landscape bloomed into beauty as the seasons and years unrolled. The farmers became specialists, and grape and tomato processing plants and canning factories were opened. Comparatively early in the century beautiful houses were built, and considering the privations experienced so recently in the struggle to tame the wilderness and somehow to make an adequate living for mere survival, it is amazing to observe how elaborate and elegant many of even the earliest houses were.

Lumbering was one of the greatest industries at first. Sawmills were operating early in the history of practically all of the towns. Flatboats and rafts were built, and cargoes, especially lumber and salt, floated to cities as near as Pittsburgh, as far as New Orleans. Hardwoods were burned and the ashes baked and sold to chemical companies. One cannot help but regret the wasteful use of timber for this purpose, although there are, after all, success stories to brighten the picture somewhat. There is the one about the merchant in Dunkirk who sold twenty to forty thousand dollars' worth of potash and pearlash during six successive years. Four such asheries in Ashville gave the town its name—and the prosperity of the town is reflected there in some of the most distinguished houses to be found anywhere in western New York.

Some of the houses that are surmounted by cupolas or captain's walks, especially near Lake Erie, were built by the colorful and intrepid captains of ships that sailed the lakes—men who could well afford fine houses since they were paid from forty up to seventy-five dollars a month. Manning ships on the lakes, however, was neither the easiest nor the safest life for their crews. A few lighthouses served as guides along the shore, but stories of violent storms and tragic wrecks with many lives lost are common in the history of the lakes—stories of vessels that went up in flames, of collisions, of plagues, and of ships that disappeared entirely leaving no trace.

The value of homes that were built was in relation to prosperity, of course—and prosperity then as now had to do with the kind of work people did to make a living. All of the fine lumber that was plentiful and cheap at that time made possible prosperous industries such as the manufacture of doors and sashes, of tubs, pails, barrels, and firkins—all much in demand. Cargoes of them were shipped down the river to Pittsburgh and to cities in the South. Worsted mills were established; tanneries were busy especially in Busti, Jamestown, Panama, and Clymer; potteries in Fluvanna, Frewsburg, Westfield, and Gerry; bricks were made in a number of places. Mirrors were manufactured in Falconer, vegetable and flower seeds raised in Fredonia, candles molded in Sinclairville and Dunkirk, and handsleds made in Frewsburg. Laona is an old town, now somewhat on the sidelines, but the first flouring mill in the county was in operation there in 1810. The making of wine started in Brocton, and this, of course, was a great impetus for the growing of grapes. Cheese factories were in Sinclairville and Arkwright; rope was made in Sheridan, and a lime kiln was there, too. In 1848 a railroad repair shop was started in Dunkirk—a necessary adjunct to that busy railroad terminal—and, shortly after, locomotives were manufactured there, with an iron works producing many kinds of machinery; bedsprings were made in Mayville.

The establishment of lucrative industries follows the history of the developing needs and later the luxuries of the people. Before 1820, in Jamestown and vicinity, there were lumbermills, gristmills, and tanneries; local industry provided pearlash, pottery, furniture, and fur hats (many of beaver, but some, surely, of raccoon); cloth-dressing and wool-carding were important enterprises. All of these activities were basic and necessary.

Then from 1820 to 1840, production saw many additions: Fanning mills, foundries, and machine shops appeared; publishing began; boats were built—horse-boats, riverboats, steamboats. A list of products of the time would include wool cloth, flannels, and ribbons; pails and tubs and firkins; saddles and harness and wagons; scythe snaths and axes; bee hives and supplies, for bees were most useful in pollinating the vineyards. A clock factory opened in Busti; and a shop in Cherry Creek made spinning wheels.

Women who were employed to spin flax in households and early factories were called "spinsters," and they earned a shilling a day. A little wheel was used for spinning flax, a big one for wool, and a loom was necessary in most families to weave cloth. The name "linsey-woolsey" we all know, but perhaps not so familiar is the fact that the material got its name because the warp was of linen thread and the woof of wool—giving it the long-wearing qualities necessary in those days.

Annals for the last half of the century show that boat-building continued to be important in the area. Other things both fascinating and functional being made at this later time were silk hats and cigar boxes; ice cream and candles; shoes and snuff; Scotch blood purifier and little Mandrake pills; wood carvings; photographic paper and plates—and dulcimers that cost about fifteen dollars apiece in Stedman. There were also pianos and organs; carriages and sleds; wheelbarrows; mattresses and upholstered furniture; church and lodge furniture; washing machines and voting machines. There were breweries and a gasworks—and electricity had arrived.[14]

Other more personal services being provided were advertised in the 1881 Atlas of Chautauqua County, where E. J. Swetland, a dental surgeon in Panama, New York, states: "Special attention given to the administering of Nitrous Oxide Gas for the painless extraction of teeth." [15] A jeweler advertised, who was also the proprietor of the Opera House; and there were attorneys, physicians, blacksmiths, liverymen, insurance agents, and a public speaker.

Many old houses have exciting tales connected with them and their part in the sad story of slaves escaping from enforced service. These escape routes may have started as early as 1804. Since the activity was illegal in every respect, the utmost secrecy was required, and, although the Underground Railroad probably existed in every northern state, it could not, of course, be organized. There could be no record made of these fugitives, of the routes they desperately traveled, or of the abolitionists and others who helped them along the way.

It is known now that one route came from Ohio and Pennsylvania to Westfield, Fredonia, Silver Creek, and on to Buffalo; another came from the south through Busti, Jamestown, Frewsburg, Ellington, Cherry Creek, to Cattaraugus County, then Arkwright and Forestville. The final problem for the fugitives was to get passage some way across Lake Erie into Canada. All of those who furnished help of any kind, even to the extent of providing a free meal, risked imprisonment and heavy fines.

There are hidden rooms in some of the attics of the houses shown in Section IV, and in barns; or there could have been dugouts extending through walls of cellars. These secret places, it is said, harbored the unfortunate refugees until a night came that was dark enough for them to slip cautiously on to the next station, or to a friendly boatman who would take them across the lake.

It would make this brief record too voluminous indeed to give an account of all the people who were important in settling and developing Chautauqua County. Proprietors of the first gristmill, the first tannery, sawmill, ashery, store; pioneer farmers, physicians, blacksmiths, tailors were each of them brave and enterprising and necessary.

But it would be unfair to name only a few of the people involved, impossible to tell about them all.

Native sons of the nineteenth century in Chautauqua County were leaders in many fields—writers, artists, musicians, philanthropists, industrialists, political leaders, merchants, educators. Of more general interest may be the nationally, even internationally, known people who lived or visited here and were well acquainted with the territory. They include Daniel Webster; Horace Greeley; William Henry Seward, Governor of New York State, Secretary of State when Lincoln was President; Major General George Stoneman; General John McAllister Schofield, Secretary of War in President Andrew Johnson's Cabinet; Reuben Eaton Fenton, New York's Civil War Governor; and William Barker Cushing, hero of the Civil War. Thomas Alva Edison came here and helped to promote the Chautauqua movement; others important in this work were Lewis Miller and John Heyl Vincent. The Merritt family, pioneers in developing iron mines in northwestern United States, knew Chautauqua County. So did George Mortimer Pullman and Laurence Oliphant; Philip Phillipps, who traveled all over the world conducting song services; and Dr. Mary E. Walker, eccentric, and only woman to be given the Congressional Medal of Honor—this for her four years of service as a lieutenant in the United States Army Medical Corps during the Civil War. Samuel Langhorne Clemens did some of his best writing here; and Grace Greenwood, Alice Jean Webster, and Grace Richmond, also famous writers, were among the noted visitors. There was David Parker, originator of the money-order system; and Richard Theodore Ely, Chairman of Political Economy at Johns Hopkins, was a well-known sojourner. Not the most esteemed, certainly, but perhaps the most intriguing visitor was Robert G. Elliott, expert electrician and, of all things, world-famous executioner.[16]

This is an imposing list, to be sure. But of much greater importance are the pioneers and the settlers who developed, defended, and maintained the county; those who, furthermore, established its character and its infinite variety—evidenced to some extent in the comfort and beauty of their homes.

III

The Architecture

Entrance to Smith Bly
house in Ashville.

The story of the building of homes and the spreading of architectural designs in western New York State follows the history of transportation there. It also has to do with people, of course: where they came from, what they left behind them, and undoubtedly with the styles of their former homes, for which, no doubt, they were more than a little homesick.

It is interesting that there seems to be very little evidence of architectural influences from the people who emigrated here directly from the Old Country. The Scandinavians, indeed, who settled, particularly in the Jamestown area, adapted very quickly to the current American architectural styles.

Early houses were built, naturally, along the old roads and the routes the stagecoaches followed. Styles were brought by the people who came by stage, wagon, or by the waterways: up the Mississippi River and east by way of the Ohio; or by the others traveling in much greater numbers from New England or coming north on the Hudson, then west by way of the Erie Canal to the Great Lakes. Some French characteristics may have come from New Orleans but, basically, designs for houses depended upon what had already happened "back east," especially in New England.

Books and periodicals publishing news, plans, and advertisements about current architecture were having wide circulation at the time. Two books that were particularly influential, both of which were written by Andrew Jackson Downing (1815–1852), will be referred to later.

A few houses of Post-Colonial architecture, built in the early years of the nineteenth century, appear in western New York, and some are shown in Section IV. They are two stories high, usually have a dignified fan-lighted doorway, and sometimes this entrance is centered, ensuring a balanced room arrangement. The end walls have chimneys on parapets, usually in pairs, to heat the sets of rooms on each side, and the cornices are designed with a repeated decorative motif.

Much of the domestic architecture of the nineteenth century in western New York, however, could be placed in two large classifications. Within the second of these, certainly, there is a world of diversity. The first, "The Romantic Era," could be dated from about 1820 to 1860 and includes the Greek Revival, the Gothic Revival—especially the Pointed Gothic—and the Italian Revival styles. Western New York has many splendid Greek Revival houses, almost as many in the charming Pointed Gothic tradition, and any number that have Italian characteristics.

The second group, dating from about 1860 to 1910, has been called confused, undecided, ostentatious—and to many people "Victorian" means all these things. This is inaccurate and actually the term "Victorian," used in relation to architecture, has no meaning at all. There were a number of fine American styles of architecture produced during these years which are vital enough to stand alone, and they will be considered in this way. The period will be called here "The Era of Variety." Within it we have the Post-Civil War house, the Romanesque Revival and the American Craftsman style. Distinguished examples of all of them will be found in Section IV.

These designs overlapped, of course, in time and in their use, so that one could very well discover almost anywhere in New York State an elaborate house with Gothic windows, finials, and other Gothic decorations; a classic pediment and columns; iron cresting; and even an Italian tower boasting a bracketed roof—all of this highly irregular but certainly picturesque. They were spacious and well built, too, and should be taken seriously. Truly, there was many a "battle of the styles"—a battle that was won in some cases by American ingenuity and taste, and lost in others with the production of conglomerate monsters.

Then there will be enchanting houses that cannot and, indeed, should not be classified at all, although their approximate dates may be found. Finding and making a record of these unusual ones is also one of the objectives in this work. Among all the houses in all classifications, only the exteriors are considered.

THE ROMANTIC ERA

THE GREEK REVIVAL

This style came to America by way of England, for it was the British architects who rediscovered the classic proportions and graceful details of the architecture of Greece for use in their own building. Benjamin Latrobe brought these ideas across the Atlantic, and their vogue swept the eastern part of the United States and the South. Not only in architecture were Greek and Roman themes popular. For a time all things classical became the fashion—interiors, furniture, clothes—even towns were given Greek names. Thomas Jefferson was a devoted admirer of Roman architecture and, more particularly, that of the great High Renaissance Italian architect, Andrea Palladio. This is clearly evident in his home at Monticello and on the campus of the University of Virgina.

Greek and Roman architecture, then, was adapted enthusiastically by American architects to government, public, and commercial buildings—with good and bad results. Frank Lloyd Wright, on one visit to St. Louis, spoke disparagingly of an office building there because a little Greek temple, he said, was perched precariously on top of its fourteen or more stories. Many of the classical designs, however, were highly successful. Because of the unity of these buildings and their monumental character, they were completely appropriate for commercial use, as well as for appearance. Talbot Hamlin, in *Greek Revival Architecture in America,* says:

> A surprising number of such buildings are still standing, still being used for their original purpose; the uniformity of their cornice lines, the monumental repetition of their granite piers, and the rhythmical regularity of their openings give a pleasant harmony and unity to the streets they border. The best of these buildings are simple, useful, unostentatious, human in scale, and restrained and delicate in detail.[17]

A tragedy of so-called progress is, however, that slowly these gorgeous public buildings are also disappearing, one of the most recent sacrifices being the imposing classic Pennsylvania Station in New York City, built as recently as 1910 and designed by the great American architects, McKim, Mead & White. It does not seem reasonable that a mere fifty-three years is the proper lifetime for such a splendid building. Aside from the fact that razing it is a wasteful extravagance, surely it could be put to some practical use —surely, indeed, beautiful landmarks such as this should be preserved.

In the Greek Revival houses, wood, stone, and brick were utilized and even sometimes a combination of these materials. The use of this exquisite style for country houses seems, perhaps, anachronistic in the rugged pioneer America of the nineteenth century. But our enterprising forebears were prosperous, they worked long hours, they wanted fine homes to return to then, just as they do now, and they considered the Greek style the most splendid—as, indeed, it was.

Hamlin tells us:

> Nowhere more than in up-state New York . . . is Greek Revival work more vital and more varied. We can point here and there to influences taken over from the earlier Massachusetts-Connecticut-Berkshire work; we can see again and again the influence of Lafever both in mass and in detail. Occasionally a name is known, like that of Cyrus Wetherill, an Englishman who came to Orleans County in 1814 and worked there till 1835, but that is almost all. Yet about the personalities, even about the ideals, of the actual designers and builders who took and merged and changed these influences and from them created individual new buildings we know almost nothing. Wherever they were, again and again they built well, and the houses they put up do much to make the character of upper New York what it is.[18]

The Greek Revival houses shown in Section IV of this book, some built of wood, others mainly of brick, are basically of two types. The more familiar and more easily recognized style has the classic portico with columns, usually two stories high. Sometimes there is a one-story wing on one or both sides—and these may or may not have porches. There is a pediment above the columns, often quite low; again, instead of the pediment there may be a hip roof sometimes surmounted by, of all things, a cupola or a captain's walk. The Doric and Ionic Greek orders were used most frequently in the columns and pilasters, and they were often fluted, with occasionally a carved decoration at the top of the shaft itself.

The second type has no portico, but these houses are even more subtly lovely with their fluted pilasters and Doric or Ionic capitals, often hand-carved. There may be wings, again, some with recessed porches; and these houses can have front gables, too, or a flatter hip roof.

In Greek Revival styles the entrance is important. Doors framed with columns or pilasters, and with the classical entablature above, frequently have exquisite carved details on the architrave or on the panels of the door itself. So-called "eyebrow" windows sometimes appear in the frieze band. Occasionally these are covered with a grille or fretwork of Greek design which could be cast-iron or even carved of wood.

There were modifications in a variety of Greek temple-like one-story cottages. There were transitional houses, too, having the basic plan—a two-story center section with one or two one-story wings. The classic portico has disappeared there, although there may be a porch with jigsaw decorations and brackets under the cornices.

Happily, a comparatively large number of Greek Revival houses are surviving in upstate New York. They were given their proper settings originally, and for decades they have been lived in and loved. One comes upon them suddenly in the most unlikely places—personal interpretations of the Greek style in houses of stately proportions, restrained detail, right in scale, and the whole having remarkable sophistication—out in the middle of what so recently was wilderness. They are found as far to the east as Ellington, to Clymer in the west, at Fentonville close to the Pennsylvania line, and all through the north and central parts of the county.

We should be, and we are, grateful for this. Thomas E. Tallmadge says, in *The Story of Architecture in America:*

> . . . whether a style is good or bad—and by that is meant logical and appropriate or the opposite—is no criterion of its importance historically, and for that reason alone every monument of the Greek Revival should be carefully preserved and honored. Aside from the regard of the historian and archaeologist, the lover of beauty for its own sake, too, would regret the loss of a single column or pediment. Absurd as these monuments may seem when judged by a logician, they are entirely satisfying to one who believes that beauty is its own excuse for being. On that side, at least, the contribution of the Greek Revival was almost without exception one of charm and dignity.[19]

THE GOTHIC REVIVAL

Hamlin says that the interest in medieval architectural design was basically caused by the popular literary romances that practically everyone was reading, also that the picturesque atmosphere of old-world castles was desired by the new rich in America for a tangible

26

expression of their wealth.[20] In any event, this romantic period brought to our country from England a revival of medieval Gothic design in churches, other public buildings also, and in residences.

An American architect identified with this style is Richard Upjohn (1802–1878), who was best known for his churches, although he designed some fine Gothic houses along the eastern seaboard that are still called "castles."

Another American architect who worked successfully in this style, James Renwick, Jr. (1818–1895), designed the lovely Grace Church, its rectory, and St. Patrick's Cathedral, all in New York City; and the familiar Smithsonian Institution building in Washington, D.C.

The ideas of the American architect Alexander Jackson Davis (1803–1892), however, were spread more widely in western New York. Among his designs are large Gothic villas, but his smaller houses were less pretentious, were artfully decorated, and had a superbly dignified quality. These picturesque small masterpieces, immediately popular, were emulated throughout the East and the Middle West by naive and much less skillful builders, resulting in the so-called "carpenter Gothic," or "gingerbread," houses with which we are all familiar. A more suitable name for them is the Pointed Gothic Style. Many are entirely successful; some were earnestly adapted to a basic Swiss chalet type of house—to a sympathetic eye, all are charming.

The widespread use of this "Country House" style, with all its embellishments and variations, was facilitated by the publication of two books by Andrew Jackson Downing before the middle of the century. The first one, illustrated, had the complete title of, *Cottage Residences; or a Series of Designs for Rural Cottages and Cottage Villas, and Their Gardens and Grounds, Adapted to North America.* It is clear from the title page that the second book was much more ambitious: *The Architecture of Country Houses; Including Designs for Cottages, Farm-Houses, and Villas, with Remarks on Interiors, Furniture, and the Best Modes of Warming and Ventilating. With Three Hundred and Twenty Illustrations.*

John Claudius Loudon (1783–1843) published in England in 1833 his *Encyclopaedia of Cottage, Farm, and Villa Architecture and Furniture,* to which Downing gave credit for ideas for country-house design, although Alexander Jackson Davis was the architect for many of the houses in Downing's books. Loudon's greatest interest, incidentally, was landscape gardening; and it was he who first designed the glazed-dome conservatories which were at one time a necessary part of the homes of the wealthy in this country. Loudon perfected the curvilinear technique of glazing which made them possible.[21]

The proper setting, the contour of the land, the gardens, were carefully considered and planned in the design of an estate. Mae C. Nairn has done much research on this home landscaping of the last half of the nineteenth century and an outline of some of her findings follows:

1. Patience was of utmost importance—planting was done for the ages! Trees were set for best possible growth—if at all possible "specimens" were brought from far places. Shrubs were massed, often with mixed harmonizing colors, and spaced for future growth even though they might look sparse for a few years.

2. Italian gardens, especially formal ones, were the inspiration of a great many homeowners.

3. Formal effects were popular and were utilized on nearly every estate.

Entrance areas were important where shrubs or trees were massed on each side or where formal gateposts were used.

Sweeping curved driveways were often lined with trees and shrubs.

Lawns were kept free and green, with shrubs placed at far edges or massed in formal effects in the center.

Terraces were greatly admired and different levels were developed —often geometrical in design.

4. "Living area" gardens stressed the natural spirit in the placing of flower beds and borders, shrubs, trees, and winding walks. They were used for relaxation and were well furnished with hammocks, lawn swings, chairs, and benches; a summerhouse often completed the picture.

5. Lawn ornaments were very popular: animals such as deer, lions, dogs made of cast-iron; picturesque urns of ceramic, iron, or clay, planted with trailing vines and flowers. Sundials and birdbaths were admired.

6. Large estates made much of outdoor games such as lawn tennis, bowling, croquet—all played on closely clipped grass. Ponds and garden pools were popular, with well-landscaped walks leading to them and perhaps to a summerhouse at the edge of the water.

7. Arbors were used everywhere, for vines, roses, grapes. Often they were developed as outdoor living rooms placed either on grass or on large, flat, embedded stones.[22]

It is futile, of course, but absorbing to consider the comparative costs for house-building that have come about within one hundred years. In *Cottage Residences,* Downing recommends "an Ornamental Farm House" with twelve rooms, which could be built with stone or timber found on the property of the owner, and should not cost more than $1700. Another, smaller one could be built of wood, he says, for $830; or a massive place in the Italian villa style "of elegant variety" would cost $7800 if balustrades were of cut free-stone, if wood, $7600. Again, he describes a tremendous "Villa of the first class, in the Pointed Style ... by A. J. Davis, Esq. of Albany." This has everything: library, dining room, kitchens, pantry, drawing room, conservatory, study, six sleeping rooms, a bathroom, a water closet, sleeping accommodations on the third floor; portecochere, carriage porch, towers, stained glass, ribbed ceilings—all this opulence and more for from twelve to fifteen thousand dollars, back in 1844.[23]

In the Downing books are pictures of many "cottages" whose cheerful offspring can be found in most of the villages in western New York. The gables and bargeboards, the edges of the roofs and the porches are trimmed with carved or sawn wooden ornaments and edgings, rich in detail and often extraordinarily fancy. He also liked a projecting roof supported by brackets, and these brackets, with the passing of time, became more and more elaborate. More tangible are some Alexander Jackson Davis houses themselves that still stand, elegant and sturdy, in eastern United States.

Although within limited areas one sees repetitions of the patterns of decoration, there is still, over all, a great variety of such designs. A study of them in detail would be a valuable part of the historical record of the architecture of the nineteenth century, for they are disappearing.

Downing recommended bay windows, porches, and the board-and-batten, or vertical-boarding, type of wood construction. He says, in *Country Houses:* "We greatly prefer the vertical to the horizontal boarding, not only because it is more durable, but because it has an expression of strength and truthfulness which the other has not." [24] Timbers, he says, grow vertically, and therefore vertical boarding is more suitable on a wooden house.

There are pleasing and well-built variations of the cottages, Swiss chalet houses, and the less ornate but larger Gothic villas originally pictured in his books, and scattered throughout Chautauqua County. Delightful examples are shown in Section IV.

HOUSES IN THE ITALIAN STYLE

In the middle years many western New York houses of brick or wood reflected influences from Italy. Here are the towers inspired by the Italian bell tower or the Italian villa—also arched windows, balconies, bays, extended hip roofs supported by brackets, ornamental lintels. The decorations are sometimes incredibly elaborate, but they are usually correct in scale, since the houses are large and basically irregular in plan.

Gable or hip roofs have the low slant typical of Italian villas; porches resemble Italian Renaissance loggias. Also in keeping with the fifteenth-century revival of interest in classical architecture during the Renaissance in Italy are the Doric, Ionic, and Corinthian orders used on columns and pilasters. Some of the finest examples of such houses anywhere in the State may be found in Chautauqua County.

ERA OF VARIETY

THE POST-CIVIL WAR HOUSE

Usually miscalled "Victorian" are the elaborate, often magnificent, houses which were built following the Civil War, when, during the Reconstruction, the trend was away from all things classical or medieval.

Too much has been said about the period's eclecticism, its confusion, its poor taste, its indecision. A more tolerant approach and more careful observation of it will surprise one with the beauties that can be discovered in these mansions. And mansions they are—spacious, livable—and building them surely must have given their owners a sense of achievement.

Theirs is a comfortable style, too, that could be added to logically—this could not happen to most Greek Revival houses which are complete in themselves—to provide for growing families and liberal entertaining. Furthermore, as John Maass states, in his *American Heritage* article "In defense of the Victorian House," "We have never given the Nineteenth Century the benefit of the doubt, yet only a thin line divides the 'vulgar and ostentatious' from the 'bold and self-confident.' "[25]

It is undeniably true that the interiors—with their elaborately heavy furnishings, bric-a-brac, rubber plants and "things" everywhere —are restless and disturbing even to think about. But it was the fashion then, and we could be reminded that in the twentieth century this vogue has even returned in a small measure. Fashion is no excuse, certainly, for unnecessary discomfort, but it is a reason for some degree of tolerance in criticism. Many of these handsome late-nineteenth-century houses are still lived in, now elegantly but simply furnished so that the fine craftsmanship of the builders shows unmistakably.

Very often scrollwork decoration has been called Victorian, as if it had been invented in the nineteenth century. Certainly it appears on houses of the period. Actually, however, the decoration was derived from Gothic stone tracery. In wood it became extremely ornate, sometimes delicate, hanging like lace from gables and repeated in shadows when lighted by the sun. It had exuberant use on Downing-inspired cottages, many designed by Alexander Jackson Davis, earlier in the century.

The elaborate decorations on the exteriors of Post-Civil War houses included cast- or wrought-iron cresting that became the new kind of ornament often replacing the wooden tracery. It decorates the edges of porches and roofs of houses and raises towers even higher with its feathery crown. The houses of this period in the collection in Section IV are almost all of brick; they are large, some have Italianate towers, many are trimmed with the wooden tracery, others with iron cresting.

The mansard roof is common, too, having come from France, where it was used by Francois Mansart (1598–1664) in the seventeenth century on his lovely Chateau de Maisons, near Paris. The Louvre, too, has a notable mansard roof. In domestic architecture here, an interesting use of this French motif is on the seemingly one-story building which is actually two stories high—indicated by the dormer windows which pierce, at intervals, the mansard roof. Another French characteristic is the building with a center tower that curves up to a cast-iron cresting.

THE ROMANESQUE REVIVAL

The Romanesque Revival was the realized vision of Henry Hobson Richardson, the great American architect who died, too young, in 1886. His splendid style flourished during the last two decades of the nineteenth century, but was not so wide-spread as were the others. Although Downing, in *Architecture of Country Houses,* pictures a "Southern Villa—Romanesque Style," [26] it was Richardson who developed the style most vitally. "He was the genius," says Wayne

Andrews, in *Architecture in America,* "who brought order to American architecture after the Civil War." [27]

His greatest works are churches, libraries, public buildings; he designed the city hall in Albany, New York. The buildings are great solid piles of tremendous dignity, characterized by arcades, colonnades, arched doors and windows, towers that are often circular with conical roofs, thick walls of stone that have highly textured surfaces. Buildings, they are, for the ages!

In domestic architecture Richardson's shingle houses represent a truly American style—vigorous, enduring. But these qualities were not achieved as successfully by lesser architects and builders when Romanesque arches and towers became parts of enormous wooden houses with high roofs, gables, porches, and portes-cochères. The required texture was obtained by using shingles of all sizes and shapes and applying them in a variety of patterns. The interiors were often unfortunately finished in golden oak, highly varnished. Here, indeed, are some of the monsters that seldom receive a kind word. Not many are found in western New York.

THE AMERICAN CRAFTSMAN STYLE

In houses of the nineties we find again shingles in a variety of shapes and patterns; bargeboard decorations are on gables that sometimes have been extended at the base to form hoods over windows below. There is a great deal of diversity in the plans of these large houses and much carpenter decoration was applied to them—in addition to the bay windows, porches, towers, and balconies. This is a lively phase of American folk art and it deserves our respect and affection.

Summerhouse in Westfield.

31

IV

The Houses

Back door of 1873 Pierce house in Fredonia.

This map of Chautauqua County is divided with a broken line into five regions, numbered one to five, counter-clockwise. The pictures that follow, then, are grouped according to village, and the villages are grouped together according to region.

Alphabetical listing of villages wherein houses are located, with the regional number of each town, and picture numbers:

VILLAGE	REGION NUMBER	PICTURE NUMBERS
Ashville	Four	88–94
Barcelona	Three	51
Bemus Point	Two	46
Brocton	Three	47–50
Busti	Five	103, 104
Cassadaga	Two	41–43
Chautauqua	Three	71
Chautauqua Assembly	Three	72–75
Cherry Creek	One	9–12
Clymer	Four	80
Dunkirk	Two	21–23
Ellington	One	13
Fentonville	Five	108
Findley Lake	Four	78
Forestville	One	5–8
Fredonia	Two	24–40
French Creek	Four	79
Frewsburg	Five	105–107
Gerry	One	14–16
Hartfield	Three	68
Jamestown	Five	95–102
Panama	Four	81–87
Point Chautauqua	Three	69, 70
Ripley	Three	76
Silver Creek	One	1–4
Sinclairville	One	17–20
South Stockton	Two	44, 45
Stedman	Four	77
Westfield	Three	52–67

Nineteenth-century horses on the way to Laona, Sinclairville, perhaps even to Jamestown, were refreshed at this Arkwright Hills spring. A concrete horse-trough replaced the old wooden one early in this century, but the clear cold water continues to flow.

Region One

SILVER CREEK

FORESTVILLE

CHERRY CREEK

ELLINGTON

GERRY

SINCLAIRVILLE

Summerhouse in Ellington.

1. Holman Vail, master shipbuilder, completed this Greek Revival house in 1835, when its size and beauty impressed everyone who came to Silver Creek. The interior woodwork originally had the interesting character of a ship's saloon, since much of it was built by the owner himself.

39

2. Seemingly it is a one-story house, but this is contradicted by dormer windows in the mansard roof, indicating the second story. The house has a compact charm, and it was built in Silver Creek during the last decade of the nineteenth century by S. S. Starring himself, who was a carpenter.

3. A most enterprising man, Oliver Lee, built this house and Lake Erie's Silver Creek harbor, too, in 1828. Lee, originally from Westfield, had walked the shores of Lake Erie all the way to Silver Creek and had discovered that here was a natural harbor. Shortly thereafter he purchased from the Holland Land Company, for $350, land which included the lake front—thus starting the village on its road to prosperity.

The porches and extension of the wing were added to the house later in the century, but the facade was in the original design, and still in use is the sterling silver hardware on the door.

4. Silver Creek's first brick house, 1842, is in the Post-Colonial style, with parapets separating the chimneys on each end, cut-stone lintels and sills, and a cornice with dentils across the front. It is similar to the Frazine house in Fredonia, but with the plan reversed.

5. This house in Forestville, built by Cyrus D. Angell, c. 1870, is classic in style and distinguished by the elliptical arches connecting the pilasters on the facade. The bay is probably a later addition. The iron fence has exceptionally handsome posts and gateway.

6. This dignified Forestville brick house is of the Post-Colonial style: an oblong two-story building with low-pitched hip roof, chimneys centered near both ends, the interest focused on the doorway slightly recessed within its fan-lighted arch. Departing from the early style, and probably added later, are the brackets under the eaves and the extended roof. The house was built about 1812 by Daniel Barber, a prosperous blacksmith, who was elected in 1814 to the office of "Overseer of the Poor."

7. Forestville's fine hip-roof house, with a cupola, dates from about 1860. The wide eaves are supported by paired brackets connected and unified by the dentil molding. The doorway, with its bracketed cornice as wide as the front panel of the two-story bay, is imposing.

8. This house was built in 1872 by Levi Pierce, who was a Forestville landowner and builder of large houses for large families—a subsequent owner of this one, indeed, having ten children. Italian are the repeated arches, the grouping of triple windows over the porch, the brackets, the tower, the circular windows—but it has a mansard roof.

9. George N. Frost built this Italian villa in Cherry Creek in about 1850; it is an excellent example of the style. It has the flat-roof tower, hip roofs, wide cornices with paired brackets beneath, and paired arched windows. The octagonal wing is also typical, and the porch is like an Italian loggia of the Renaissance. The small arched windows in the transom over the doorway are sometimes called "tombstone lights."

10. American craftsmanship is well illustrated on this Cherry Creek house, with its emphasis on the vertical line. The rectangular bays paneled below and above the windows, the brackets, and the balcony with its hood, lead upward to the pierced bargeboard decorations in the gables—unusually lacy and delicate. Large half-circle designs with many spindles are used here, and again, on a smaller scale, on the porch, where the quarter circle connects the top of the posts with the soffit grille.

11. This 1845 farmhouse was built by another Frost—George H.—
who, it is said, "sheltered and fed alike the traveler and the fugitive
slave." [28] He came to Cherry Creek when bears and wolves roamed
freely in the almost unbroken forest, cleared his land, and worked
it into a prosperous farm. The handsome doorway with its bracketed
pointed entablature is a collector's item—its low slant repeated on
all the window heads.

12. Rich bargeboard ornamentation on all gables distinguishes the American Craftsman house in Cherry Creek. The pierced decoration is finely detailed and is designed to frame the paired windows geometrically, but the stalactite edging has a subtle curve in its contour, flowing down almost to the ends of the gable. Again, this curve forms arches at the top of porch openings, where the stalactite motif is repeated in the design of the brackets below the porch cornice. The decorations are used on side gables and on the cupola, and a band of shingles traces the line of the porch roof.

13. This Greek Revival house, built in Ellington about 1849, has Ionic pilasters that rest on stone plinths, separated by stone steps below each window and the door. In the hip-roof wing, the columns are Doric.

14. Small, oblong, hip-roof, center chimney, recessed porch—thus briefly may this Greek Revival house in Gerry be described; and all that can be remembered about it is that it is over a hundred years old. However, the classic doorway, the frieze grilles, the proportions will always lend it an air of distinction.

15. Gerry's 1877 house was built by Hiram Seers. There is a careful difference in the sizes of the brackets and pendants to fit the different roofs: the cupola, the bays, and the house roof itself. The modillions vary, also, to suit their locations. This attention to detail is most satisfying.

16. The large Tuscan villa in Gerry has an ornamental band across the tower that ties in with the cornice lines of the two wings. The gables have a low slant, and the roof, it will be noticed, becomes level at the eaves. The paired windows within an arch, shown at the front gable end, were called Florentine arched windows. The house was built in about 1870 by J. Newell Wilson, a prosperous lumber dealer. The porch, of course, is comparatively recent.

17. The Greek Revival house in Sinclairville, built in 1840, has wide
antae, in keeping with the heavy entablature and cornice. The window
heads go through to the interior.

18. There seems to be no record of one of the most interesting and, indeed, most beautiful of the Greek Revival houses in Chautauqua County. Perhaps it speaks for itself and needs none. It lies in serene isolation on top of a hill two miles north of Sinclairville—red brick throughout except for decorative grilles and cut-stone lintels, sills and base trim; and nobly proportioned with full-length windows, recessed doorway, brick pilasters, and paired brackets under the hip roofs. Originally, the lowest wing on the left was repeated on the right. No contemporary architect could design a finer, more charming one-story home.

19. The oldest house in Sinclairville was built about 1810. The thick stone walls, and windows whose lower sashes are not as high as the upper ones (twelve over eight), are indicative of its age.

20. The Copp house in Sinclairville, c. 1853, has all the engaging qualities of the Gothic Revival Pointed Style with its emphasis on the vertical: board-and-batten siding, steep gables topped by finials (here there are nine gables including the dormer windows and hooded doorway), lovely curved Gothic-style windows throughout the second floor, and Gothic lights flanking the doorway; there are twin chimneys and, finally, elaborate tracery everywhere. A New York City architect built three or four such houses in the county, no two alike, but his name is not known.

Region Two

DUNKIRK

FREDONIA

CASSADAGA

SOUTH STOCKTON

BEMUS POINT

Summerhouse in Dunkirk.

21. There is satisfying unity achieved by the repetition of the Roman arch in this Dunkirk house, built about 1855. From the first floor Italian loggias with their Corinthian columns, paired in front, and the arched doors and windows throughout, to the segmental arching of cornice and cupola with its Palladian windows—it is completely self-contained. The house has always been owned by members of the Fullagar family, who entertained notable people here. One of the most dazzling was Princess Louba Louboff Rostovsky—Lady-in-Waiting to the Czarina of Russia—who had the good fortune to marry into the Fullagar family.

22. This 1819 Dunkirk house was built by the first physician there, Dr. Ezra Williams, with lumber taken from the property itself. The roof supports are still covered with bark and the huge hand-hewn uprights are held together with pegs. The house is the classic farmhouse type with two massive chimneys unusually placed in the center, on each side of the gable. The porch was added in 1900.

23. The 1868 house in Dunkirk has a mansard roof, a spectacular collection of sharply pointed gables—twelve, at least—and a tower surmounted by fine cast-iron cresting. Interesting details embellish this thirty-room house: the medieval trefoil opening in the side-wall gable, the stone trim above the window openings, and the ornamental band below the cornices of the tower, roof, and bay. The house has always been owned by the Williams family.

24. The G. Nelson Frazine brick house in Fredonia, c. 1835, is a splendid example of the Post-Colonial style. Characteristics of this rather severe early nineteenth-century mode, clearly indicated, are the two stories, parapets that rise flush with the end walls composed of paired chimneys connected with a platform, three windows, and a cornice with dentils across the front.

25. This handsome Greek Revival mansion was built in Fredonia in 1855 by Noah Snow. The splendid portico has irregularly spaced Ionic columns, and there is an Ionic colonnade along the side wing. For the main part of the building, locally made bricks were used, but the cupola, with low hip roof, is of wood. The house stands adjacent to the college campus. The State University of New York has acquired it to be the residence of the president of the College at Fredonia.

26. This back view of the Snow house shows the possibilities for successful additions to a Greek Revival house.

27. & 28. The 1840 Octagon House in Fredonia has walls twenty-four inches thick that are made of grout—an incredibly hard material. A scattering of octagon houses, built around this time, extended through the Midwest, a very few as far west as the coast, but many are found in New York State. This property is one of the few on which the octagonal barn, or carriage house, survives.

29. Three Greek Revival houses were designed for the Fredonia Risley family (the family that started the famous Fredonia seed business in 1834) by John Jones in about 1837, and two of them remain standing. This one, for William Risley, has a two-story central portico, porticos on flanking wings, and fine Doric fluted columns. The entrance is generous in scale, provided for by irregular spacing of the front openings, and the recessed doorway has side and transom lights.

The Anna Jones house, the Fredonia Episcopal Church, and other houses and buildings in Fredonia and Westfield, not identified, were also designed by John Jones. He was born in Wales, came to this country and settled first in Westfield then, in 1837, he moved to Fredonia, where he lived until his death in 1852.

30. The Elijah Risley, Jr., house—next door to the William Risley residence—Greek Revival of the Doric order designed by John Jones, has one wing, and the hip roof is surmounted by an interesting but incongruous captain's walk. Elijah, Jr., started the first grocery store in Fredonia.

31. In 1835 architect John Jones designed this Greek Revival mansion for his daughter Anna—although, actually, it is a redesigned older house (c. 1806). It has a hip roof, a portico with five Doric columns, a handsome doorway, and ornamental grilles in the frieze band. There is a portico in back, also, with Doric columns. The house has been moved a mile or so from its original site in Fredonia.

32. "Eyebrow" attic windows pierce the frieze band of this one-story Greek Revival house in Fredonia. The property was a Holland Land Company purchase, and the building dates from about 1820. An early owner had ambitions to raise silkworms—and the mulberry trees are still there.

33. It was not unusual for square columns to be used on Greek Revival houses. They are surely correct here, since the same lines appear on the pilasters and the massive entablature over the entrance to the recesssed doorway. This well-proportioned small house, c. 1845, in Fredonia was purchased by Luther Webster in 1859 for $950! Mark Twain visited here, and in the family appears the name of Jean Webster, author of *Daddy-Long-Legs*.

34. This splendid villa, with its tower, arched windows, its handsome doorway, and the Palladian window set in the mansard roof, is a composite style of great dignity. The ornamental drip-stones are, indeed, carved stone. The house was built in the sixties in Fredonia.

35. Basically Greek Revival of the temple type with flanking wings
—but transitional in detail—is this house, c. 1850. It was built by
Ulysses E. Dodge who, in 1867, was Master of the Grange in Fredonia—the very first Grange organized in this country.

36. The charming midcentury Glisson house in Fredonia, built snugly against the hillside (suggesting a Swiss chalet) is trimmed with bargeboard decorations, restrained in design. The lower level, only, is of brick, and it has solid posts, while the balcony porch in front has an ornamental pierced wood balustrade, and the posts, too, are pierced.

37. The 1840 Elias Forbes house in Fredonia is a picturesque example of the Gothic Revival Pointed style. The wooden tracery decorations were not confined to the front—they are consistently used on all sides—but they are all different in detail. The little square room in the L is a late addition.

38. The house of John Forbes, brother of Elias, also in the Pointed Gothic style, has a particularly fine pointed window, with curved sides, in the front gable. The brackets on the five-sided porch are elaborate, and the pierced wood balustrade also has a carefully detailed design.

39. This must have been an imposing Fredonia estate when the house was first built—dominating its own wide acres—where even the barn was designed to harmonize with the house. Most of the elaborate details appear on the roof, and here the ornate brackets are unusually large, the chimneys are extremely handsome, and the distinguished cupola is surmounted by a finial.

40. The Joel J. Parker house is a strange and interesting interpretation of the Greek Revival style. Slim fluted Doric columns are irregularly spaced on the recessed porches on each side; the wooden entablature has an unusually wide frieze board; there are cut-stone lintels and a gently sloping hip roof—all these well-organized classic details distinguish the midcentury house. Mr. Parker was a fruit and vegetable grower in the town of Fredonia.

41. & 42. Harmony and good proportions still prevail in this neglected house of the Pointed Gothic style in Cassadaga. Wooden scrollwork and its shadow trim the steep gables, whose arched windows are dramatized by the sunburst background. The pattern of the roof shingles lends a soft texture; an ogee moulding finishes the porch window and door heads.

43. That the midcentury Denny mansion in Cassadaga harbored runaway slaves can well be believed. It is big enough, certainly, to have any number of hideaways; and the circular windows in the mansard roof in the tower, they say, were splendid lookout posts.

44. In South Stockton is this fine midcentury Tuscan villa with arched windows—triple groups on the gable ends—bays, roof that flattens at the eaves and with paired brackets beneath. The mansard roof on the tower is not unusual in houses of this kind. This impressive place is not a town house—it stands at a crossroads in an entirely rural area.

45. This small early cottage, a plank house, was built in South Stockton in about 1810. The decorated porch, added later, is completely in harmony.

46. The Rush house at Bemus Point, built shortly after midcentury on land purchased in 1815 from the Holland Land Company, has an arcaded L-shaped porch decorated with delicate columns, refined carvings, and brackets—as lovely as any to be found in the county.

Region Three

The entrance to Westfield's Hinckley house showing details of iron trim on door- and window-heads and sills, with particularly handsome iron railings and posts.

47. Captain James Butler, master of ships sailing the Great Lakes, built this mansion in Brocton about 1870. Cast-iron cresting once decorated the edges of the tower and the porch roofs—these, however, are not the original porches. Not many of the elaborate finials such as the one soaring above the octagonal tower still survive, and even this one is not perfect: the tip used to carry a weathervane.

48. The irregularity in contour of this 1894 house in Brocton is compensated for by its great size. There are sixteen rooms, and the complexity of gables and projections give a good idea of their variety and shape. The sunburst in the porch pediment, on the porte-cochere, and over some of the windows, was a popular motif—as was the circular tower with its pointed roof. The barn stood handy, and the ornamental gazebo was necessary for civilized living.

49. & 50. An American craftsman used a great deal of decoration on this 1888 house in Brocton, and it cost $6500 to build. All corners of the house are beveled, and there are decorated hoods over the second-floor diagonal windows. The mill work was probably done locally, since the same designs, in a variety of arrangements, appear on other houses in the area. The porte-cochere is especially lacy, and notice should be taken of the gable ornaments on the handsome barns. The larger one on the right, much older than the house, was originally a stable paved with wooden bricks, where a change of horses was made on the stagecoach run.

51. In 1829, when the tide of settlers was surging to the west through the Erie Canal, the Barcelona Lighthouse was built, serving also as a beacon for Lake Erie sailing ships. It was a natural-gas light—someone has called it "the tallest gaslight in the world." When the stone building was planned, careful specifications covered all details, and it was to cost no more than $2,700; then, upon its completion, Joshua Lane was appointed by President Andrew Jackson to be the lighthouse keeper. He was paid $350 a year for this service. The lighthouse was abandoned in 1857, but was relighted in 1962 by the town of Barcelona. The house has been somewhat modernized.

52. This 1820 Greek Revival Westfield house, unusually wide, has
a handsome recessed entrance with square columns below the well-
proportioned entablature. The floor of this porch is one huge block
of stone that extends a few feet in each direction under the house.
The Farrington family, who were prosperous farmers, built this place,
and it stayed in the family for many years.

53. The Eason house in Westfield, c. 1835, was built on the site of an 1806 log cabin. Motifs from different styles are used here, probably added at different times—an extended roof with brackets, a pointed window under the center gable, a classic entrance with its crown of iron cresting—but they all combine agreeably to make an attractive home.

54. The 1830 Tennant house in Westfield was designed by architect Elias Barger for Austin Smith. Lawyer Smith became the first principal of the Fredonia Academy, now the State University of New York College at Fredonia. With its fine Ionic columned portico and doorway, and balanced side wings, the house is one of the finest Greek Revival mansions in the State. Descendants of the original owner still live here.

55. This midcentury Gothic Revival house is in Westfield. The triple front gables are steep and trimmed with bargeboard traceries that are rhythmic and quite delicate. Slim finials surmount the center gable and those on each side of the house. The Gothic entrance and the straight-sided Gothic triple window above are particularly handsome. At one time there was a porch—the iron balcony was added later.

56. The ornate but dignified Hinckley house was built in Westfield
in 1851. The two paired arched windows on the first floor balance,
with size and importance, the entrance; and the window sills and
drip-stones above all arched openings are cast-iron in an elaborate
design. Even the chimneys have arched panels, and the iron railings
are based on a fancy arched pattern.

57. The 1838 house in Westfield is an imposing example of the Greek Revival style. Two bays form the front portico, instead of the usual three, and the arched fan-lighted door is balanced on the opposite side by a window of similar design. An elaborate balustrade surrounding the balcony is repeated along the second-floor porch on the side.

The house is interesting historically: it was built by William H. Seward, Governor of New York State in 1841, who later became President Lincoln's Secretary of State during the Civil War. He lived here but three years, when it was bought by George W. Patterson, last agent of the Holland Land Company, who also served as Lieutenant Governor of the State of New York.

58. Corinthian capitals top the pilasters and square porch columns on this unusual Italian Renaissance Revival house in Westfield and paired brackets serve as transitional elements to the hip roof. Another porch in back, and paneled and bracketed chimneys, complete the fine design. When it was built in about 1864, the walls were sanded and finished to resemble stone blocks.

59. Mr. Joe Tinney came to Westfield in 1832, started the first tin shop, invented the tin bake-oven for use in fireplaces, and lived in this hip-roof house. Then, during the 1840's, a group of Millerites occupied it and used the second-floor, perfectly square room, to await the end of the world.

60. Presently the home of the Chautauqua County Historical Society, the McClurg Mansion, completed in 1820, was built by the resourceful Scotch-Irish pioneer, James McClurg. The booklet about it, published (undated) by the society, reads in part: "He fired his own lime, made and baked his own bricks, prepared woods from local timber for the interior, secured skilled bricklayers and carpenters, bringing them from Pittsburgh up the rivers and lake to Mayville by boat, and by portage to Westfield." They tell us, too, that the design was inspired by a castle that McClurg had known back in Ireland. The stepped gables and chimneys with their decorative brick work are especially handsome.

61. The board-and-batten front part of this Westfield house was added in 1866 to a much older section, by George P. York, owner of an iron foundry. Based on the Gothic Revival Pointed style, the building has straight-sided Gothic windows in the steep gables, framed by lacy bargeboard decorations. Twin chimneys are centered on the roof.

62. Unlike any other discovered in the County is this unique brick house built in Westfield in about 1829, supposed to have been copied from one the family left in England. Philip Lou Stephens had nine sons, and this industrious family planted the first grape vineyards in Westfield west of Chautauqua Creek. The arched recessed porches, the main one with a balcony, the decorative brick design under the cornice, give the house great distinction.

63. This Westfield Gothic Revival Pointed style brick house, c. 1840, has straight-sided pointed drip-stones over paired windows and elegant tracery in the center gable. The extensions to the house, added in back, show how efficiently additions could be made to houses of this style.

64. Built in 1853 by Dr. John Spencer, designed by architect Elias Barger, this splendid house continues its useful life as Westfield's Memorial Hospital. The original cast-iron trimming remains on the front porch and balcony balustrade, but gone is the canopy that extended over the three center second-floor front windows. A pair of engaging iron dogs still guard the approach to the house.

65. This villa in Westfield has lost its center tower but interesting architectural details remain: the repeated arches within arches in windows and doors, the arcaded porch with handsome drops substituting for posts in the front sections, the second-floor canopies repeating the roof design of the bays, and the original iron cresting. The house was built in 1874 by Isaac Cochrane.

66. Reuben Wright left Westfield for California in 1849. In 1855
he journeyed back East—laden, more or less, with gold—by way of
a ship sailing around the Horn. To complete a fine success story: in
1870 he returned to Westfield and built this twenty-room mansion.
Its three stories embody a lively collection of porches, balconies,
gables and complex roofs surmounted by splendid paneled chimneys.

67. George Washington Patterson devoted much of his life to the improvement of Westfield—its water and light systems, its roads and trolleys; and he subsidized, also, the building of the Westfield Library. His fine twenty-two room mansion, built about 1880, has unusually elaborate brackets and interesting two-story pilasters that bind the angles of the side bay.

68. Men by the name of Barnhart and Scofield founded a small village near Mayville which derives its name from their names: Hartfield. The small Greek Revival house there has a hip roof, attic windows in the frieze band, and decorative carvings over the door and windows. It is a plank house, and it was built by Barnhart before the middle of the century on the Plank Road.

69. The gables of a plain two-story cottage were richly ornamented with elaborate decorations, thus dressing it up so that the house was quite fashionable for the last decade of the nineteenth century. Located at Point Chautauqua, across Lake Chautauqua from the Assembly Grounds, it hopefully reflects the spirit of that popular place.

70. Point Chautauqua's Bonnieview Hotel, c. 1880, somewhat out of context here, nonetheless has such richly imaginative decoration that its opulence should be recorded. Now but a shadow of what it used to be, it is obvious that soon even the shadow will become a memory—and probably not even that for long.

71. This is a Chautauqua house in the Italian style, large and fine, with a central tower surmounted by a finial. (An especially interesting aspect of this study is the location of some of the houses. One would expect that such an elegant one as this, for instance, would be within or very close to a town. But it stands quite alone, surrounded by magnificent old trees, and there does not seem to be another house within miles.) All details here are consistently handsome: the arcaded porch, the segmental arch over all windows and the curved glass window panes, the brackets and an especially elaborate one beneath the canopied main entrance.

72. Carpenter craftsmen were busy indeed in the Chautauqua Assembly grounds during the nineties. Tracery forms the arches of this porch —more delicate than the design of the balustrade around the one above—and bargeboard decorations are in all the gables.

73. American folk art in architecture is vividly expressed in this Chautauqua Assembly "tent" house. The rafter ends under the eaves are decorative, and the elaborate arch, dominating the bargeboard in the gable, frames the balcony door with its fancy pointed doorhead. Balconies are important in this sociable community and this one has interesting spindle designs in the balustrade, repeated around the porch and above the porch openings.

114

74. One should see from all sides this fabulous house that faces the lake in the Chautauqua Assembly grounds. But notice here the many gables, the vertical timber construction, the paired columns, the decorative bargeboards, brackets, and balustrades. In the back there is a tower, semi-detached, large enough for a room on each floor. The building shown next to this house was erected in the twentieth century.

75. Seldom, or never, are there two houses alike in the Chautauqua Assembly grounds. This one, with the usual balcony, has a rhythmic trim around the gable with the anthemion motif in the apex, while the entire gable itself contains a finely textured design. The pierced-wood porch decorations are elaborate and intricate, and their contours form arches that are quite different from the arcade of the balcony above.

76. The Ripley house, with its interesting textures and its round towers and porch capped with conical roofs, could have been inspired by Richardsonian architecture. It lacks charm, certainly, but this house, and others similar to it, are part of the history of American nineteenth-century houses.

Region Four

STEDMAN

FINDLEY LAKE

FRENCH CREEK

CLYMER

PANAMA

ASHVILLE

Water pump on the back porch
of Panama's Gothic Revival house.

77. Close to the small village of Stedman (near Panama), this Greek Revival cottage of unusual quality was built early in the 1850's for Aiken Hiller by a carpenter, George Losee. The entrance, it will be noticed, is on the one-story side portico, which has a pent roof supported by five Ionic columns.

78. The Findley Lake house, built with an interesting treatment of levels to follow the contour of the land on the lake shore, has a low pitch to its hip roofs. The decorative panels on the bays, harmonizing with the arched windows, are pleasing and suitable. The porch, the main opening of which is higher than the others, is probably a later nineteenth-century addition; the balustrade and grille patterns have a clear-cut charm.

79. Front gables, separated by the recessed entrance, are features of this **Pointed Gothic** house in French Creek. The bargeboard carving is quite lovely—heavy but rhythmic—and there are pierced-wood decorations on the porch.

80. Clymer's Greek Revival house has antae paneled to the base, and they are decorated at the top with the anthemion motif.

81. Panama, N. Y., has been called an American Athens: look closely at most of the nineteenth-century houses there and you will see a Greek temple. This well-proportioned Doric mansion, with handsome doorway and hip-roof wings, was built for Dr. Cornelius Ormes and is one of the few houses whose architect is known. John Capple was the versatile architect, as well as the contractor and builder, in 1833.

82. This, one of Panama's charming Greek Revival houses, has always been in the Randolph family since it was built in 1842. The heaviness of the frieze board is pierced and lightened with attic windows. The porch, doubtless a later addition, hides the center entrance with its wide lintel, and partly covers the antae, which are decorated at the top with the anthemion motif. The second-floor front windows have been placed closer to the center than those on the first floor, to make room for the heavy cornice and entablature.

83. & 84. Sardius Steward admired Greek Revival houses. He lived
in this one, c. 1840, in Panama before he moved to another one in
Ashville. The mansion here (probably designed by the Panama architect, John Capple) is falling to pieces; but the lovely carved designs
above the windows and on the entablature over the beautiful doorway,
the Ionic fluted columns, the classic proportions, still survive as re-
minders of its former glory.

85. Another Steward house in Panama was built about 1827. The Ionic scrolls are larger than usual, owl-like, and the design is much simplified on the pilasters and on the Ionic columns flanking the entrance. A wood-carver and carpenter named John Newhouse worked on some of these Panama houses, and local tradition has it that he carved Greek-style columns out of solid tree trunks. He may have interpreted other Greek motifs, also, in his own way, and they may appear, unidentified, on some of the houses in this area.

86. The Panama Gothic Revival house with vertical board-and-batten construction, elaborate scrollwork, finials, and pendants, would have been admired by the inventor of the style: A. J. Downing. Part of the tower, originally another story high with a castellated top, was removed early in the twentieth century.

87. This Greek Revival house in Panama was known as the Horace Glidden house and was built about 1850. The two-story facade carries Ionic pilasters and it had, originally, a fine entrance flanked by Ionic columns with a recessed door. However, the entablature is still decorated with carving and the handsomely detailed mouldings. The long, one-story wing with its Ionic colonnade is distinguished by the unusual band of carving above the doors and windows of the porch.

88. The Smith Bly hip-roof house which was built in 1835 in Ashville at a cost of $7000—an appreciable amount in those days—is a nearly perfect example of Greek Revival architecture. The impressive entrance has a carved architrave supported by Ionic columns that are repeated in a colonnade along the one-story wing. Ionic pilasters and carved lintels over the first-floor windows—to match the door space, the windows are longer than those on the second floor—also are handsome details. Workmen were brought all the way from Philadelphia to carve the woodwork.

89. The Sardius Steward house in Ashville, built by Samuel Brown
in 1853, is part of an estate originally transferred from the Holland
Land Company in 1819, to one James McClallen, for a "considera-
tion" of $652.15. It is Greek Revival with slender Doric fluted col-
umns and a narrow entablature.

90. This handsome place in Ashville, built about 1835 by Amariah
Atherly, was surely an expression of American confidence. There was
no dearth of imagination here: the sawn designs of the pendant finish
on the cornices of the front- and back-porch gables, the lower side
porch, the balcony, the entire roof, and, finally, the cupola are *all*
different! There is also variety in the shapes and decorations of the
arches (suggesting Moorish design) on all porches—front, side, and
back—in the pierced designs of the columns, and in the balustrade
and pedestals of the balcony. Flamboyant, perhaps, but inventive;
and harmony was somehow achieved.

91. Back view of the Atherly house. A "rags to riches" story is told about a young runaway boy from Pennsylvania, Jim Camel, who came to Ashville in the middle of the nineteenth century, fell in love with the Atherly mansion, and vowed that one day he would own it. Years later, James Campbell (spelling his name correctly now) struck oil, came back to Ashville, bought the house, married, and lived happily ever after!

92. Included on the Atherly estate is this house and a lovely small church. In the middle of the cemetery nearby is a shaft inscribed: "Erected as a family monument A.D. 1850—a legacy of D. L. Atherly."

93. One of the oldest houses in Ashville, shown here, was built in 1824 by the town's first physician, Dr. Vine Elderkin. The brick was hauled by oxcart from Buffalo; the lintels and door frame are cut stone. Inside, the walls are plastered directly onto the brick, and the carved woodwork is cherry.

94. Well proportioned, handsomely detailed, is this Greek Revival house near Ashville, c. 1860. It is symmetrically designed, with identical wings on each side of its center entrance. Notice the coherence achieved by the curve that connects the lines of the antae with those of the pediment. The anthemion motif on the antae is similar to but not identical with other such carvings on houses in the county. The lines of the doorway, with its imposing entablature, are marred, of course, by the shutters.

Region Five

JAMESTOWN

BUSTI

FREWSBURG

FENTONVILLE

Two-story Doric columns on the back of the 1890 Jamestown house.

95. William Hall built this distinguished Greek Revival house in Jamestown in 1846. A prosperous farmer for many years, he later helped to finance Hall's Alpaca Mill, run by English operators with imported English machinery. The imposing hip-roof house has a handsome portico with Doric columns and antae, side and transom lights in the doorway, decorative grilles in the frieze band.

96. The Jamestown house, c. 1890, is eclectic—and interesting. Irregularly spaced pilasters are used in a bold way that is highly effective. The Doric columns of the portico are flanked by square paneled ones, and a triglyph appears in the entablature above each one. The semicircular windows and the pediment are in the classic tradition. The back of the house has a porch and balcony that are dramatically connected with great two-story paired Doric columns.

97. Ionic columns on the portico and wings, Ionic pilasters, and a gracious center entrance—all are perfectly balanced in this wide and handsome Greek Revival mansion in Jamestown. It was built in 1848 and is supposed to have been designed by architect Oliver P. Smith. Nathan Breed, the original owner, could well afford this fine home, since he operated the flourishing cradle and snath factory there. Incongruously, a second story has been added to one wing.

98. The Hall house in Jamestown was designed by architect E. G. Dietrich and built in 1896. It combines characteristics of houses of other times with an eclectic use of varied motifs. The two porticos with the slim two-story Ionic columns—four in front, three on the side—are imposing.

99. The Tew house in Jamestown, built about 1885, should be
studied in detail, for there is a lot to see here. The mansard roof has
remarkably picturesque dormer windows; there are two distinctively
different towers, one with finials; decorative are the cornices, the
shingle pattern on the roof, the brick corbel band, the bands of cut
stone connecting windows and walls, encircling the building. One
should notice, also, the three stepped windows indicating the location
of the stairway inside—a medieval idea. The porches, of different
styles, were probably later additions. The third floor, originally, was
a ballroom in which a dais was built especially for the grand piano.

144

100. A late nineteenth-century house in Jamestown, embodying some Richardsonian ideas, has gambrel roofs, two medieval round stone towers with conical roofs, and a balcony with a Gothic arch. The house was designed during the last decade of the century by architect E. G. Dietrich.

101. This Greek Revival house near Jamestown dates from about 1840. A number of other houses, similar in style, were built not too far from this one. The wing, here, is a recent addition.

102. Reuben Eaton Fenton, Representative in Congress, Governor of New York State, United States Senator—Chautauqua County's most famous nineteenth-century citizen—built this fine midcentury Tuscan villa in Jamestown. Italian are the square tower, wide projecting eaves, roofs that are almost flat, decorative brackets, arched windows, projecting bay, and arched loggia. A statue of Governor Fenton stands on the pedestal in front of this dignified building.

103. This board-and-batten Gothic cottage is called by the Busti townspeople "The House of Seven Gables." So-called "drip-stones" or label mouldings, but in wood, decorate the tops of both the first-floor square-top windows and the particularly handsome second-floor windows, which are curved Gothic. Even the barn windows have the Gothic shape. Well-placed quatrefoil medallions on the house serve as decorations.

104. The Greek Revival Root House in Busti, c. 1835, has remarkably beautiful details. The Ionic fluted pilasters are tapered; the
dentils in two well-proportioned sizes are introduced in the pediment,
and are repeated in the architrave surrounding the building (not just
in front) and in the lintel of the classic doorway.

105. In 1833 George Washington Fenton built this engaging story-and-a-half Greek Revival house on Ivory Road outside the town of Frewsburg. Enhanced with Ionic pilasters and a classic doorway, it is surrounded by venerable trees. A hidden scuttle-door to the attic could be evidence of the truth of the story that the house was a station for the Underground. The porch was added in 1914.

106. In this Frewsburg house, c. 1830, there is a happy mixture
of details of different styles. The central mass, with classic recessed
doorway, has a wide gable and is flanked by recessed wings with
porches, similar to a Greek Revival design. Added later are the
rhythmic bargeboard tracery ornaments, the brackets, and front and
side porch posts and decorations. A handsome house, it belonged to
the Fenton family—Reuben Fenton lived here before he became
Governor of New York State.

107. Frewsburg was named after its first settler, John Frew, and this house was built by his nephew James, in 1821. The porches and wing undoubtedly were later additions.

108. The Greek Revival hip-roof house in Fentonville dates from about 1840 and was occupied by William Henry Harrison Fenton, brother of the Honorable Reuben E. Fenton, Governor of New York State in the sixties. The ornamental frieze over the entrance is elaborately carved, the Ionic capitals of the pilasters are carefully detailed too, and the recessed door has well-proportioned paneling and side lights.

Notes and Bibliography

Sleigh, c. 1855, with wrought-iron details—in Sinclairville.

$\mathcal{N}otes$

INTRODUCTION

1. Wayne Andrews, *Architecture in America* (New York, Atheneum, 1960), preface.

2. Thomas E. Tallmadge, *The Story of Architecture in America* (New York, W. W. Norton, 1927), p. 36.

SECTION I

3. Clayton Mau, *The Development of Central and Western New York* (Dansville, N.Y., F. A. Owen, 1958), p. 179.

4. Andrew W. Young, *History of Chautauqua County, New York* (Buffalo, Matthews & Warren, 1875), p. 471.

5. *The Holland Land Company and Canal Construction in Western New York*, Buffalo-Black Rock Harbor Papers, Journals and Documents (Buffalo Historical Society, 1910), p. 387.

6. Young, *op. cit.*, pp. 151-152.

7. *Ibid.*, p. 80.

SECTION II

8. Emory F. Warren, *Sketches of the History of Chautauque County* (Jamestown, N.Y., J. Warren Fletcher, 1846), p. 40.

9. *Ibid.*, p. 41.

10. Charles J. Shults, ed., *Historical and Biological Sketch of Cherry Creek* (Charles J. Shults, 1900), p. 163.

11. O. Turner, *Pioneer History of the Holland Purchase of Western New York* (Buffalo, Jewett, Thomas & Co., Geo. H. Derby & Co., 1849), p. 577.

12. Gilbert H. Hazeltine, M.D., *The Early History of the Town of Ellicott* (Jamestown, N.Y., Journal Printing Co., 1887), p. 353.

13. William J. Doty, ed., *The Historic Annals of Southwestern New York* (New York, Lewis Historical Pub. Co., 1940), Vol. 1, p. 309.

14. *Ibid.*, pp. 348-359.

15. *Historical Atlas of the County of Chautauqua, N.Y.* (New York, F. W. Beers & Co., 36 Vesey St., 1881), p. 26b.

16. Doty, *op. cit.*, pp. 386-395 .

SECTION III

17. Talbot Hamlin, *Greek Revival Architecture in America* (New York, Oxford, 1944), p. 149.

18. *Ibid.,* p. 270.

19. Tallmadge, *op. cit.,* p. 117.

20. Hamlin, *op. cit.,* p. 332.

21. John Gloag, *Victorian Taste* (New York, Macmillan, 1962), p. 41.

22. .Mae C. Nairn, "Research Notes on Landscape Gardening" (unpubl., 1963).

23. Andrew Jackson Downing, *Cottage Residences,* 2nd ed. (New York, Wiley and Putnam, 1844), pp. 89-171.

24. Andrew Jackson Downing, *The Architecture of Country Houses* (New York, D. Appleton, 1854), p. 51.

25. John Maass, "In Defense of the Victorian House," *American Heritage,* Vol. 6 (October 1955), p. 36.

26. Downing, *The Architecture of Country Houses, op. cit.,* p. 353.

27. Andrews, *Architecture in America, op. cit.,* p. 32.

SECTION IV

28. Shults, *op. cit.,* p. 165.

Bibliography

Adams, Ellen E. *Tales of Early Fredonia*. Fredonia, N.Y.: *Fredonia Censor,* 1931.

A Guide to the Empire State. Compiled by Workers of the Writers' Program of the Works Projects Administration in the State of New York; Sponsored by New York State Historical Association. New York: Oxford University Press, 1940.

Anderson, Arthur Wellington. *The Conquest of Chautauqua*. Vol. 1. Jamestown, N.Y., 1932.

Andrews, Wayne. *Architecture in America*. New York: Atheneum Publishers, 1960.

Case, Victoria, and Ormond, Robert. *We Called It Culture*. New York: Doubleday & Co., 1948.

Chautauqua County Historical Society Booklet on James McClurg House, undated.

Crocker, Elizabeth. *Yesterdays . . . In and Around Pomfret*. Fredonia, N.Y.: *Fredonia Censor,* Vol. 1, 1960; Vol. 2, 1961.

Darrow, Floyd L. *History of the Town of North Harmony*. North Harmony, N.Y.: Town Board, Vol. 1, 1953; Vol. 2, 1955.

Doty, William J. (ed.). *The Historic Annals of Southwestern New York*. 3 vols. New York: Lewis Historical Publishing Co., 1940.

Downing, Andrew Jackson. *Cottage Residences* (2nd ed.). New York and London: Wiley and Putnam, 1844.

————. *The Architecture of Country Houses*. New York: D. Appleton and Co., 1854.

Edson, Obed. *History of Chautauqua County, New York*. Boston: W. A. Ferguson & Co., 1894.

Gloag, John. *Victorian Taste*. New York: Macmillan Co., 1962.

Golden Yesterdays 1805–1955. Poland (N.Y.) Sesqui-Centennial Program, 1955.

Hamlin, Talbot. *Architecture Through the Ages* (rev.). New York: G. P. Putnam's Sons, 1953.

————. *Greek Revival Architecture in America*. New York: Oxford University Press, 1944.

————. *The American Spirit in Architecture* (Vol. 13 in "The Pageant of America Series"). New Haven: Yale University Press, 1926.

Hazeltine, Gilbert H., M.D. *The Early History of the Town of Ellicott.* Jamestown, N. Y.: Journal Printing Company, 1887.

Historical Atlas of the County of Chautauqua, N.Y. New York: Beers Publishing Co., 36 Vesey Street, 1881.

Hitchcock, Henry-Russell. *Architecture, Nineteenth and Twentieth Centuries* (Pelican "History of Art Series"). Baltimore: Penguin Books, 1958.

Hurlbut, Jesse Lyman. *The Story of Chautauqua.* New York and London: G. P. Putnam & Sons, 1921.

Jackson, Joseph. *American Colonial Architecture.* Philadelphia: David McKay Co., 1924.

Kimball, Fiske, and Edgell, George Harold. *A History of Architecture.* New York and London: Harper and Bros., 1918.

Loudon, John Claudius. *Encyclopaedia of Cottage, Farm and Villa Architecture.* London: Longman, 1833; new ed., 1846.

Maass, John. "In Defense of the Victorian House," *American Heritage,* Vol. 6 (October 1955), pp. 34-41.

————. *The Gingerbread Age: A View of Victorian America.* New York: Rinehart & Co., 1957.

Mau, Clayton. *The Development of Central and Western New York.* Dansville, N.Y.: F. A. Owen Publishing Co., 1958.

McKee, Harley J. *Architecture Worth Saving in Onondaga County.* New York State Council on the Arts, Syracuse University School of Architecture, 1964.

McMahon, Helen G. *Chautauqua County, A History.* Buffalo: Henry Stewart, 1958.

Nairn, Mae C. *"Research Notes on Landscape Gardening."* Unpublished, 1963.

New Topographical Atlas of Chautauqua County. Philadelphia: William Stewart, 1867.

Peat, Wilbur D. *Indiana Houses of the Nineteenth Century.* (Indiana Historical Society publication.) Chicago: R. R. Donnelly & Sons Co., 1962.

Schmidt, Carl F. *Greek Revival Architecture in the Rochester Area.* Scottsville, N.Y.: Schmidt, 1946.

————. *The Octagon Fad.* Scottsville, N.Y.: Schmidt, 1958.

Schuyler, Montgomery. *American Architecture.* New York: Harper & Bros., 1892.

Scully, Vincent J. *The Shingle Style.* New Haven: Yale University Press, 1955.

Shults, Charles J. (ed.). *Historical and Biological Sketch of Cherry Creek.* Published by Charles J. Shults, 1900.

Starr, Sylvia, and Wertz, Joseph B. "Architecture that Came from Athens," *House and Garden,* Vol. 64 (July, 1933), pp. 49-51.

Tallmadge, Thomas E. *The Story of Architecture in America.* New York: W. W. Norton & Co., 1927.

The Holland Land Company and Canal Construction in Western New York. (Buffalo-Black Rock Harbor Papers, Journals and Documents.) Buffalo: Buffalo Historical Society, 1910.

Thomas, David. *Travels Through the Western Country in the Summer of 1816* (Auburn, 1819), as quoted in Mau, *op. cit.,* pp. 176-180.

Turner, O. *Pioneer History of the Holland Purchase of Western New York.* Buffalo: Jewett, Thomas & Co., Geo. H. Derby & Co., 1849.

Vaux, Calvert. *Villas and Cottages.* New York: Harper & Bros., 1857.

Warren, Emory F., *Sketches of the History of Chautauque County.* Jamestown, N.Y.: J. Warren Fletcher, 1846.

Williams, Henry L. and Ottalie K. *A Guide to Old American Houses 1700–1900.* New York: A. S. Barnes & Co., 1962.

Young, Andrew W. *History of Chautauqua County, New York.* Buffalo: Matthews & Warren, 1875.